# I Can't Recall Exactly When I Died

# I Can't Recall Exactly When I Died

Poems by

Diane Elayne Dees

© 2025 Diane Elayne Dees. All rights reserved.
This material may not be reproduced in any form, published,
reprinted, recorded, performed, broadcast,
rewritten, or redistributed without
the explicit permission of Diane Elayne Dees.
All such actions are strictly prohibited by law.

Cover design by Shay Culligan
Cover image by Oormila V. Prahlad
Author photo by Diane Elayne Dees

ISBN: 978-1-63980-752-9

Kelsay Books
502 South 1040 East, A-119
American Fork, Utah 84003
Kelsaybooks.com

# Acknowledgments

Thank you to the following publications, in which versions of these poems previously appeared:

*Atticus Review:* "How to Clean a House"
*Autumn Sky Poetry DAILY:* "Storm Warning"
*Gravel:* "Yard Work"
*Poetry Breakfast:* "The Final Divide," "My Ex and I Empty the Storage Unit"
*Poetry Super Highway:* "Gardening Made Easy," "The Year of No Christmas Tree," "Nomenclature"
*Snakeskin:* "Renovation"
*Sparks of Calliope:* "The Grief of Trees," "The Last Cat," "Sleeping in a New Bed"
*SubtleTea:* "The Last Time I Felt Connected to My Body," "Pulling Brian," "Loneliness of the Short Distance Sledder"
*Thimble Literary Magazine:* "Trimming the Tree Alone"

# Contents

| | |
|---|---|
| Gardening Made Easy | 11 |
| How to Clean a House | 13 |
| Renovation | 14 |
| The Last Time I Felt Connected to My Body | 15 |
| Seeking My Inner Clementine | 16 |
| The Year of No Christmas Tree | 18 |
| The Final Divide | 19 |
| Christmas Eve Day, a Year After | 20 |
| Trimming the Tree Alone | 22 |
| After | 23 |
| The Mirror That Is You | 25 |
| The Sounds | 26 |
| Corona of Fragmentation | 27 |
| On the Occasion of My Wedding Anniversary | 34 |
| Storm Warning | 36 |
| To the Crape Myrtle in My Yard | 37 |
| The Grief of Trees | 38 |
| Pulling Brian | 40 |
| Loneliness of the Short Distance Sledder | 41 |
| The Last Cat | 42 |
| Playing Tennis with My Ex | 44 |
| Nomenclature | 45 |
| Sleeping in a New Bed | 46 |
| My Ex and I Empty the Storage Unit | 48 |

# Gardening Made Easy

Stare at the blank space where violet
salvia once swayed against tall grids.
Let yourself cry for the giant pink
lilies that used to mark your homecoming.
Surrender to the army of young lubbers
that will devour every amaryllis
in sight, and feast on desserts of daylilies.
Stop deadheading; the bees won't miss you.

Come to terms with the myth:
Weeding, pruning, feeding, watering,
dibbling, and spraying are not therapeutic.
Your back hurts. You're on your own;
the other person doesn't notice,
doesn't care, how growth gets strangled
from neglect. He doesn't see how
the landscape has gradually changed
because he never knew its beauty.

Hire a landscaper and a divorce lawyer.
Invite your friends to dig your plants.
They won't take enough—no worries,
the landscape man will run a Bush Hog
right through your yard. Narcissus, gingers,
agapanthus will vanish in a blue
and yellow flash. The giant rose
that threatens your house will be cut down
just in time to dig the sewerage line
because your very existence is backed
up to a time you no longer recall.

Make a practice of not looking.
When you least expect it, elephant ears
mysteriously seed themselves in your
back yard. A pot of lantana, never
watered, lays pats of butter
across your driveway. A lone rain lily
stands defiantly pink where
the miniature rose bed used to be.
You don't offer food, you cannot
provide care. Something will live
or it will die. You are not God;
you are not even a gardener.

# How to Clean a House

First, remove the clueless husband
and toss the bulky furniture
out with him. When you can see
the walls again, paint them mauve,
sky blue, soft rose—the colors of peace.
Sell your jewelry, but keep your wedding
ring—the sledgehammer is still
in the garage. Give away your books,
cull the CD collection, remove
the pens and paperweights, donate
the dishes, pick up the rugs,
toss the wedding photos.
Hang the art you stored for years,
and breathe. Luxuriate in the space,
breathe again. Your relief will be profound,
but even with all that space, you will
trip and stumble over the pain
in every room. There is probably someone
who wants the pain, but this is an issue
that transcends donation pickups,
eBay, and even the landfill. The pain
belongs to you, and your only hope
is that there is now enough space
for the two of you to live together.

# Renovation

As our marriage crumbled,
as you treated both me and our house
with equal neglect, the mold appeared.
We learned that a wall could collapse;
the room was torn down and rebuilt,
the foundation was shored.
Finally, the ancient windows were replaced.
The workers polished the exposed ceiling beam,
providing an illusion of stability.
With the new walls, fresh paint, and newly polished floor,
the rebuilt room made all the other rooms look even worse
than they had before. You bragged to our friends
that you had chosen the marble-swirl finials,
then you canceled our vacation.
With the mold gone, I could breathe again,
and with clean lungs and dry eyes,
I canceled our marriage.

# The Last Time I Felt Connected to My Body

Was it the time that I sat close enough to view
the ornamental stitching on Midori's
gown as she offered me Sibelius
like a sacramental goblet at an altar?
Was it when I heard the metronomic swinging
of two rackets as the green clay formed fine dust?
Or when black and white surrealistic photos
made me feel like I might drop in a dead faint?
Perhaps the time I held a large sledgehammer
and transformed my wedding ring into debris.

My body has an instinct to survive,
to eat and drink and sleep through fitful dreams,
to push and pull and press and lift and sprint.
It doesn't seem to have much need of me,
or who I thought I was before I noticed
that the long-term trauma that we called our marriage
had vaporized what some might call my soul.
Will we ever meet again, I and my body?
Or have I wandered so far from the living,
I cannot seek my bones, my breath, my blood.

# Seeking My Inner Clementine

If I could forget we married, forget we ever met,
forget you never answered me or looked me
in the eye, forget you walked a block ahead of me,

forget you found a way to dismiss my every
dream, crush my joy, revile what I admired—
If I could forget you let our moldy house erode,

and sat silently while I swept and dusted, cleaned,
and did the laundry, cooking, thinking, feeling—
forget you made sure every chore you did, you left

unfinished—If I could forget all your lies,
the way you had no memory of anything
you ever said or did, the way you ruined

every party, dinner, concert, night out—
If I could forget the sleepless nights, body aches, raging
thyroid, crippled brain, the ravage of exhaustion,

who would I be? I might be another man's wife,
and when he poured himself a glass of wine,
he would also pour one for his beloved.

He would watch a movie with me, he would know
there were flowers blooming in our yard, and even
know their names. He would understand when

I stared, speechless and stunned, at art on a museum
wall. I might be another man's wife, or another man's
friend, or someone that I used to be. I might even

be myself, and not a ghost-woman whose wounded
body trudges on without her. Would I even know her,
this vital creature, free of pain with no need to forget,

or would she be a stranger—someone I vaguely
recall from a time when sleep was peaceful,
and dreams erased detritus from my mind?

# The Year of No Christmas Tree

In the year of no Christmas tree,
the husband departed in November.
Outside, the atmosphere changed
abruptly, and wrapped me carelessly
in twisted strands of humidity and oppression.
Words lost their meaning. Words like
tradition, celebration, evergreen, marriage.

In the year of no Christmas tree,
I slept on the floor of my office
and listened to frogs and crickets,
relentless in their harmonies,
suddenly mournful in their melodies.
A lamp, some alder cones, a stone egg
I bought on a trip to the beach,
*The Book of Common Prayer*—
these objects my only protection
from an abyss of my own creation.

In the year of no Christmas tree,
I wandered around the house
searching for my lost joy,
waiting to receive the gift
of release. Colored lights poured
over the neighborhood,
but illumination escaped me.
I saw myself carelessly unwrapped,
unwanted and barely acknowledged,
assigned to a dark, abandoned space—
too sturdy for the trash heap,
too broken to be re-gifted.

# The Final Divide

Tables and lamps were hauled away,
crystal and jewelry sold, bank accounts
drained, photographs banished from sight.
Meanwhile, in the attic, two crumbling
boxes of Christmas tree ornaments
remained. Months passed before
I remembered them. So we sat on the floor—
two wounded creatures among
the shimmering detritus of years
of failed holidays. You, who could barely
stand the sight of a Christmas tree, took a cat,
a clock, some gifts from me. I took two,
the rest went out with the trash. I wept
for all the tense Christmas mornings,
the gifts I never wanted, the elegant
dinners shared by two strangers bound
by contract and fear. But the next morning,
I brought the trash in, found the discarded
objects, and added some to my tiny
collection. My memories are mournful,
but the ornaments are beautiful,
they belong to me, and I claim them, knowing
only too well how easily they can break.

# Christmas Eve Day, a Year After

The first Christmas we were apart,
just weeks after you left the house
with the giant tabby and the Siamese mix,
the china, the crystal, the dark, bulky furniture,
and your steadily dripping leak of rage,
I was numb.

I don't remember what I felt, what I did,
what I ate and drank. I basked in the darkness
of the unwanted psychic vacation booked
when everything falls apart, when no one—
least of all, yourself—expects anything of you.
There was no tree, no dinner, no cats rolling
in wrapping paper. There was only stillness,
and a kind of grim relief.

A year has passed. There are blank spots
because the walls shake when the handyman
hammers in the torn-up bathroom, and art
has to be stored under the bed. I see
the empty hooks and cannot make sense
of the blank spaces. The two remaining cats
sleep on either side of the silver pillow,
carelessly guarding the abstractions beneath them.

I believe I'm going to die soon, or that
I have already died, but my brain has misplaced
the signal to direct my body to fall down.
Every time I turn on the kitchen light,
I feel an electric jolt. Sometimes sparks fly,
and I jump back, amazed that I can experience shock.
Not normally the type to plan meals,
I have spent the week cooking—a batch of polenta,
a pot of lima beans, a week's worth of oatmeal.
My rogue body goes on without me.

Today, I polish the tables and bookcase and buffet.
I take my time rubbing a pair of old rosewood
chairs, careful not to get wax stuck in the Shou
symbol that presses between my shoulder blades
when I sit. I run my fingers over the ridges of longevity;

I do not feel the blessing. All around my neighborhood,
the houses smell of pine and cinnamon. My house

overwhelms with the antiseptically sweet perfume
of beeswax and lavender. I am not quite numb,
yet I can do no more than stare at blank walls
and admire the gleam of wood that has survived decades
of supporting the weight of unnamed survivors.

# Trimming the Tree Alone

I turn off the unholiness that is cable news
and cue the music, but it's all wrong—
endless notes strung like garlands
of wrecked memories, love songs, breakup
songs, dance songs. Silence is worse,
so I settle on the eternal balm of Laura Nyro.
Then "Lonely Women" comes on, and I rush
in to fast-forward to the next song.
I pick up the four cat stockings and hesitate:
Two have died, the others live with my ex.
I let the sadness pass, and hang the red
and green stockings in their honor.
My tree is small this year, it doesn't take long
to fill it with frosted cones and assorted
ornaments—some meaningful, some new,
a few heavy with the fake snow
of my icy marriage. At the top, I place
an angel. She is simple in form, made of straw,
with no eyes, nose or mouth. I, too,
am a faceless angel, trying to get high
on a Stoned Cold Picnic while I lean in
to inhale the pure perfume of balsam.
It's just a Christmas tree. I know that,
but a ritual is a ritual, and I am trying—
—against all odds, to be evergreen.

# After

After you've hired the trainer,
changed your hairstyle, painted

the walls, bought a new wardrobe,
rearranged the furniture—

after you've risked new nail colors,
bought new shoes, discarded the mattress,

sold your jewelry, met with your bankers,
purchased better bras, changed the dinnerware—

you luxuriate in the mauves and orchids
and teals and brightness of it all.

You are a new woman. The problem
is that the former woman—the younger,

broken one—is still there, admiring your
pencil skirts while mocking you

for thinking you could ever leave her
behind. She covets your freedom,

you desire her youth. The cleverly colored
house isn't big enough for the both of you;

you bump into each other at every turn.
Will she ever move out, you wonder,

or—after you've cried all your tears
and exhausted all your rage, after

you've stopped cursing reality—
will you just forgive her and let her be?

# The Mirror That Is You

Though you are no longer here,
the mirror that is you is hung
on every wall of this house.
I cannot hide it, break it, sell it,
or give it away. I am like Elsa
in the Magic Mirror Maze;
I see myself distorted, I see myself
too clearly, I see myself through
broken glass. There is no mirror
that magnifies my flaws like
the mirror that is you. If I dare to look,
I see a woman so conflicted,
so ambivalent, so frightened
of her future—she makes a bargain
with her better self. She doesn't know
she has made this bargain—
does that make her innocent?
In the Magic Mirror Maze, no one
is innocent; everyone is a victim.
I am neither innocent nor guilty;
I stand shattered into pieces
in the mirror that is you.

# The Sounds

Sometimes, I think I hear the key turn,
the back door open, the clink
of your jacket zipper on the chair,
the thump of your briefcase
on the tile floor.
I remember the sounds
of your homecoming:
the splash of wine on glass,
the droning of the news anchor,
a gathering of loud, hungry cats.
If you spoke at all, it was to them,
or to deliver a traffic report. A hard
drive whirred, cats groomed, the host
challenged his guests, and the voice
inside my head screamed:
*Why am I here?*

Then you were gone, and all the noise
gone with you. The house grew quiet,
like the dead, but the voice in my head
grew louder: Why am I here, listening
to the labored breathing of ghosts,
missing the sound of the key in the door,
stunned by the panic alarm thumping
of my heart's requiem drumbeat?

# Corona of Fragmentation

1.

I can't recall exactly when I died;
my heart, though crushed, kept beating in good time,
my blood still coursed through all my veins. My mind
protected me from all the ways you lied.
It happened slowly; I changed from a bride
to someone who was desperate to find
escape—a book, a chore, a glass of wine,
my poems, or my garden. When I cried,
I told myself to think of things less painful,
while ignoring all the pain my body carried.
And now I can no longer recognize
the woman who was vital, smart and hopeful—
the woman who I was before we married.
A woman's soul, when stifled, slowly dies.

2.

A woman's soul, when stifled, slowly dies,
while her body, despite pain, goes on with life.
For her body still recalls when she was wise
and strong and light—before she was a wife.
She walks and talks and types; she even bleeds
the same blood as before. I know: my heart
still beats, my lungs still fill, my flesh still needs
a touch that doesn't trigger rage or hurt.
The rest of me resides in a penumbra
of who I think I might have been before
I entered our grim contract. Is it a slumber,
or is my soul a casualty of war?
I look for her, this woman I once knew;
I wonder if she's searching for me, too.

3.

I wonder if she's searching for me, too—
the self who disconnected from my body.
In what unseen terrain does she wander?
Or did she die and render me a zombie,
sleepwalking through what used to be a life?
I know I look and sound just like the woman
who lived and thrived before I shared my self
with someone who was so bereft of substance,
he had to pillage mine. I couldn't leave;
I lost my will, my courage, lost my mind.
I stayed until I knew that I was dying,
a woman with no self, no joy, no life—
a victim of a desperate psychic vampire,
surviving day by day on scraps of hope.

4.

Surviving day by day on scraps of hope,
I learned to concentrate on little things:
the pleasure the first sip of coffee brings,
the feel of water, steam and fragrant soap,
the bursts of color framed on pastel walls.
I rid my house of things that I no longer
needed; my desire for space was stronger
than my quest for nourishment or sleep or pills.
My body—swollen, burning, stiff with pain—
became my reference book. I checked its pages
for signs of grief, despair, or sudden rages;
I read its tales of trauma, loss and shame.
The book my body wrote became my guide,
exposing feelings that I couldn't hide.

5.

Exposing feelings that I couldn't hide,
my body, old but strong, went on with living
the only life it knew. My brain was slow,
my legs were fast, my appetite intact;
my resting limbs refused to settle down.
I did the things I used to do—I cooked
and cleaned, I went to work, I lunged and pressed.
Sometimes I passed a window and I saw
a reflection of my body. Then I knew,
without a doubt, that we had parted ways.
Who was this, masquerading as myself,
embodied and pretending to belong?
My small frame screamed the pain of this lost spirit,
a woman neither dead nor of the living.

6.

A woman neither dead nor of the living
can roam about as if she were still whole;
the lessons that I learned about surviving
throughout my life prepared me for this role.
Since functioning is valued as a treasure
above all else, this ghost-woman can pass
as human. By my culture's steady measure,
my dressed-up essence covers up my loss.
I wonder, if I crumbled into pieces,
how many parts of me I'd recognize.
A fractured woman's vital process ceases;
exactly what do all her parts comprise?
I haven't crumbled yet, but every day,
I search for all the parts that fell away.

7.

I search for all the parts that fell away,
and wonder if they still belong to me,
or maybe—like a weathered autumn tree—
in time, I'll have new growth I can display.
My youth is gone. My confidence, my hope,
may come to me again—I can't be sure.
The waiting and the doubt must be endured;
each passing season forces me to cope
with change, and all my shattered expectations.
I can't remember who I used to be,
and who I am is still a mystery.
I struggle not to fade in resignation,
and though, through all the tearful fog, I've tried—
I can't recall exactly when I died.

# On the Occasion of My Wedding Anniversary

On a cool Saturday afternoon
in late October, people walked
through the park in scary costumes:
witches, monsters, vampires.
I was dressed as a bride,
the most frightening costume
of all. In the autumn of my life,
it was my first time to wear it.

The wedding singer had a message:
"To bow and to bend we shan't be ashamed."
The officiant asked "Do you like her?"
After we said the vows, I turned around
to find myself alone, the groom halfway
down the stairs. The priest stepped forward,
grabbed him by the lapel: "Don't you leave her!"
I detached, not even stopping
to wonder what the guests must think.

I stayed that way for years, watching
the groom walk away again and again.
Finally, bowed and bent beyond recognition,
I saw what I had become: I was the zombie
bride, no longer a character in costume,
but the real thing—bloodless, empty,
lurching toward my own demise.

Now I am no longer bound
by contract or by vows; but rather,
I am bound by memory, which
chokes me like a malevolent fog
as it seeps into my house, my thoughts,
my cells. In the movies, zombies
prey on the living. But in real life,
we walk among you, harmless,
our blood depleted, our spirits lost.

# Storm Warning

Hurricane lilies are known to mark abandoned
homesites. Mine burst into bloom today.
This sudden storm of scarlet is so random,
a pool of blood where there should be decay.
I had no nurture left to give to gardens
or to myself. You left my landscape dry,
my heart infertile, my bones bereft of carbon,
a blossom unattended, bound to die.
When you lived here with me, you never gave
a thought to the fragility of lilies.
Now a rush of crimson leaps out from a grave,
the sky is dark, the nights are growing chilly.
The blood-red blooms foretell the violent weather,
while ice still forms from when we were together.

# To the Crape Myrtle in My Yard

I planted you more than twenty years
ago, soon after I married. I watched
you grow tall as I felt myself shrink.
Eventually, you bloomed, while I struggled
to breathe in the tiny space that had become
my life. Then I was here alone, and you
blossomed more than ever, while—deprived
of light and nurture—I wilted even more.
Finally, you came into full, glorious bloom,
only to have one rainstorm bend you
to the ground. Burdened by your own beauty,
you now bow to the earth, spilling fuschia
finery onto the lawn. You may never stand
straight again, you may even crack
and break, but you did what I cannot do—
you stood higher than the chaos all around
us, and came into the fullness of yourself.

## The Grief of Trees

Joined at the root, two tall pines
form a "V" that reaches toward the sky.
Their marriage, an inosculation,
is forever. Each is allowed to grow,
yet they never leave each other,
for their foundation is strong.

They once had a child—
a gnarly vine with bark
that stayed close to the parents,
while—like all children—
it explored the environment,
swaying in the breeze.

But breezes became strong winds,
and—over time—the trees lost
their offspring. The mighty pines
continued to sway and grow,
though who can discern
when a tree is grieving?

Not far from where the bereft gemels
stand, I, too, had a partner,
and hoped to grow while rooted
at our base. But the wild wind
of betrayal weakened our structure,
and an ice storm blew through
and detached us. No child was lost
in our storm, for there was never a child
to lose—an unseeded forest is also a loss.

Who can discern when a tree is grieving?
I grieve for them, and I observe them,
as they continue to thrive, joined securely
at their base, able to withstand the winds
that tear down the framework of those
whose roots do not reach deep into the earth.

# Pulling Brian

He mounts the sled and offers me the cables.
I take the handles, pull the slack, and fall
back while squatting low, then slowly rise.
The muscles in my legs and hips take over,
and suddenly, I'm pulling twice my weight.

My trainer's a big man, the sled is heavy,
yet each time, it's a rhythmic, fluid journey.
This comes as no surprise: I pulled a man
through years of broken vows and shattered nerves,
through crazy-making stories, gaslit lies,
sadistic plots, dismissal, and neglect.
I pulled him until part of me was dead.

I cannot see behind me. Now I'm forced
to trust the man I'm pulling to protect me.
I slowly breathe into the pull and pray
that when I've gotten past the final line,
he will not let me crash into a wall.

# Loneliness of the Short Distance Sledder

Three times a week, in pain or not, I kneel
on one knee, poised to push a weighted sled
a hundred fifty yards. I rise and thrust
the sled across the turf, my back a board,
my feet like springs. My eyes stay on the sled,
bright yellow skidding past the worn white lines.
My lines are also worn and blurred. It feels
I'm pushing years and decades as my heart
rate climbs; a broken heart pumps on and on,
though I can't feel the heat of my own blood.
I push past all the lies you told, the lies
I told myself, the nights I didn't sleep,
the joy you crushed. I feel the weight as I
push on, with leaden legs, to the last line.
I catch my breath, my heart slows down, and once
again, I realize that I'm alive.
I take the weights off, put the sled away.
My heart, I keep—I may need it someday.

# The Last Cat

The last cat left this world today;
his tender Siamese heart gave out,
his blue eyes closed one final time,
just months after his brother died.

His tender Siamese heart gave out;
he really hadn't been the same
the months after his brother died.
We knew the end had finally come.

I really haven't been the same
since both of them moved out the day
we knew the end had finally come.
A marriage ends, cats are divided—

both of them moved out that day
while the sisters stayed and lived with me.
A marriage ends, cats are divided—
and things would never be the same.

The sisters stayed. They lived with me,
we learned to master new routines.
Though things would never be the same,
we made a peaceful, cozy home.

I learned to master a new routine
when cancer came for both of them.
It was still a peaceful, cozy home,
but they were always symbiotic—

so when cancer came for both of them,
they died, as they had lived—together.
They were always symbiotic,
but I had to manage twice the grief.

The brothers died—almost together;
those blue eyes closed one final time.
And I gave up on the math of grieving
when the last cat left this world today.

# Playing Tennis with My Ex

The wind keeps shifting, putting me off
balance. The sun obscures my view
on the deuce side, and I cannot see
the ball as I toss it. My serve, already weak,
is based more on hope than competence.
We cannot find a rhythm; we look like fools,
unable to keep the ball inside the lines,
powerless to hold on to an advantage.
He aces me, I pass him. I hit drop shots
because I know him: he will not ever move
forward. We break each other again and again;
he loses his sole, but goes on with the game.
He defeats me. We pack our belongings
and go our separate ways, not even bothering
to calculate our impressive collection of faults.

# Nomenclature

I want to name nail polishes the way
Jenna Hunterson named her pies:
I'm Coping Thank You *wine,*
My Hair Is Still Everything *silver,*
I Got Good Money for That Ring *gold,*
Embarrassed I Fell for Your Nonsense *blush,*
Obfuscate This! *clear coat,*
My Lawyer Could Beat Up Your Lawyer *blue-black,*
and on casual days, when I need to just chill out—
You'll Never Again See Me *nude.*

## Sleeping in a New Bed

We hadn't had the bed that long
when the marriage ended.
I'd had the legs cut down,
knowing that he wouldn't notice.
When he moved out, I had them
cut down again because my body
craves intimacy with the vibrations
of the earth. It was solid ash,
stained mahogany—durable,
but highlighted by that red-brown
tint of blood. I changed
the wall color, the art, the lamp,
the nightstand, the bedding.
The room became an oasis
of serenity, but no amount
of mauve and gray could
calm the fires of my mind
or ease the stiffness of my limbs.

But once disassembled, the bed,
a neat pile of glossy boards,
lost its power. Now I sleep
on a new bed. The wood
is a lighter tone, the headboard is solid
and sturdy. I am still close to the earth,
but I no longer lie on layers of sorrow,
betrayal and regret. A new bed
has no magic power to heal my mind
and body, but its clean, minimal
design whispers a message
as each day ends: Keep it simple,
feel the earth beneath you,
realize your strength, and—
at long last—let your body rest.

# My Ex and I Empty the Storage Unit

Across the street from a graveyard,
the building, with its rows of dark green
vaults, reminds me of a morgue.
Inside our space, my wedding dress lies
in a long box covered by an old sheet—
a simple, inelegant casket.
We load it, along with all the bins
and boxes, into his car, and drive
to my house, a house we once shared.
Something perverse in me
wants to open the box, unwrap
the tissue, and take one last look
at this most delicate of costumes.
But I leave the lid on, alert my charity
of choice, place the box on my porch,
and proceed with the errands of the day.
When I return, the porch is clear,
the casket has been carried away.
Sometime in the not-too-distant future,
a petite woman in a well-cut vintage dress
will walk down a flower-adorned aisle,
and say vows. And while a dry cleaner
will have removed any remaining vestige
of my cells, both my ambivalence
and my hope will cling to her skin
as she glides into the unknown.

# About the Author

Diane Elayne Dees is the author of the chapbooks, *Coronary Truth* (Kelsay Books, 2020), *The Last Time I Saw You* (Finishing Line Press, 2022), and *The Wild Parrots of Marigny* (Querencia Press, 2022). She is also the author of four Origami Poems Project microchaps, and her poetry, short fiction, and creative nonfiction have been published in many journals and anthologies.

Diane, who lives in Covington, Louisiana—just across Lake Pontchartrain from New Orleans—also publishes Women Who Serve, a blog that delivers news and commentary on women's professional tennis throughout the world. Her author blog is Diane Elayne Dees: Poet and Writer-at-Large.

www.ingramcontent.com/pod-product-compliance
Lightning Source LLC
Chambersburg PA
CBHW030917170426
43193CB00009BA/883